T0401499

HA!
HA!
HA!
HA!
HO!
HA!
ROTFL!
HA!
HA!
HEE!
LOL!
SCHOOL BUS
LAUGH!
OUT!
LOUD!
HA!
HA!
HA!
HA!
HA!
HA!
HEE!
HA!
HO!
HA!
ROTFL!
HA!
HA!
HEE!
LOL!
SCHOOL BUS
LAUGH!
OUT!
LOUD!
HA!

For more laughs get these other LOL books now:

ISBN: 978-1642502343

Squeaky Clean Super Funny Knock Knock Jokes for Kidz

ISBN: 978-1642502329

Squeaky Clean Super Funny Jokes for Kidz

ISBN: 978-1642502381

Squeaky Clean Super Funny Riddles for Kidz

LOL!

Written and illustrated by Craig Yoe

Coral Gables

Published by Mango Publishing Group, a division of Mango Media Inc.

Cover Design: Craig Yoe and Clizia Gussoni
Cover illustration: Craig Yoe
Layout & Design: Elina Diaz

For permission requests, please contact the publisher at:
Mango Publishing Group
2850 S Douglas Road, 2nd Floor
Coral Gables, FL 33134 USA
info@mango.bz

For special orders, quantity sales, course adoptions and corporate sales, please email the publisher at sales@mango.bz. For trade and wholesale sales, please contact Ingram Publisher Services at customer.service@ingramcontent.com or +1.800.509.4887.

Squeaky Clean Super Funny School Jokes for Kidz

Library of Congress Cataloging-in-Publication number: Has been requested
ISBN: (print) 978-1-64250-236-7, (ebook) 978-1-64250-237-4
BISAC category code JUVENILE NONFICTION, Humor / Jokes & Riddles

Printed in the United States of America

LAUGH!
OUT!
LOUD!

HA!

contents
A+
Why did the
chicken
HA!
HA!
HA!

Chapter 1

Pencil: I don't like the new guy here in the book bag!

Eraser: Why not?!

Pencil: He acts like he's our RULER! :)

Teacher: Brenda, you have your shoes on the wrong feet!

Brenda: But they're the only feet I have!

Where's a good place to start a school vegetable patch?

In the kinder-GARDEN!

Dad: What do you have to write your term paper on?

Lad: A piece of paper!

How did the flag outside the school greet the students each morning?

It always waved! :)

Q: What does a balloon hate in school?

A: Pop quizzes!

Sue: What did the doctor study at school?

Stu: You tell me!

Sue: Blood tests! LOL!

Which superhero orders broth in the school cafeteria?

SOUP-erman! :P

What did the student carry her books in when she went to dental school?

A back-PLAQUE!

Why did the kids take their chairs out the door?

Because the teacher told them to take their seats! ROTLF!

What did the music teacher tell the bee?

BEEHIVE yourself!

Q: Why did the teacher scold the dog?

A: It didn't eat its homework!

What animal got in trouble in school?

The CHEETAH! LOL!

History teacher: Where was the Declaration of Independence signed?

Griffin: You tell me!

History teacher: At the bottom!

Hal: Why does orange juice do so good in school?

Sal: It can CONCENTRATE! LOL!

When is a yellow textbook not yellow?

When it's READ!

Knock! Knock!

Who's there?

Canoe!

Canoe who?

CANOE help me do my math homework?

Teacher: What day of the week ends with the letter Y?

Student: Yesterday?

Moe: In which class are notes the most important?

Joe: I give up!

Moe: Music class! :P

Q: Why did the kid do her homework in a tree?

A: Her mom said she needed to get higher grades!

Marmalade + Trout = Jellyfish!

Geography Guffaws!

Fred: What's the funniest thing in geography?

Ned: That's a HILL AREAS question!

Mike: Which state got the best grades in school?

Ike: Alabama with four As and a B!

Music teacher: What's your favorite rock group?

Geography teacher: Mt. Rushmore!

Teacher: What's the capital of Mississippi?

Alexis: The M!

School Snack Attack!

Why was the grape sad?

It was in a jam!

What are a school librarian's favorite veggies?

Quiet PEAS!

What do you call a bear with no teeth?

A gummy bear!

Ned: What is a scarecrow's favorite snack?

Ted: My mind is blank!

Ned: STRAW-berries!

What's a duck's favorite snack?

Peanut butter and QUACK-ers! :D

And what's a dog's favorite snack?

PUP-cakes!

Chapter 2

Math Mirth

What did the geometry teacher bring for lunch?

A SQUARE meal!

Larry: Who came up with the idea of fractions?

Mary: I don't have a clue!

Larry: Henry the $\frac{1}{8}$th!

What does a math student like for dessert?

PI!

Teacher: If you had six pieces of candy and your sister asked for three, how many would you have?

Robin: Six! ROTFL!

How do you make 7 even?

Take the S off the front of it!

Jill: Our new math teacher is odd!

Lil: She's a number that can't be divided by two!?!

What is a dog's least favorite school subject?

Mathema-TICKS!

In what state do students score highest in arithmetic?

MATH-achusetts!

Q: How did the student strain her back doing arithmetic homework?

A: She was carrying all those numbers!

Moe: Why did the boy wear glasses for his arithmetic test?

Joe: I can't even guess!

Moe: Because glasses help with d'vision!

Joe: LOL!

Where do you get three-foot-long measuring device?

At a YARD sale!

Mary: What's a math student's favorite season?

Gary: I don't have a clue!

Mary: SUM-mer! LOL!

What did 8 say to 0?

You forgot to wear your belt!

School Vacation!

Where did the joke book go for vacation?

New YUK City!

Why did the elephant have to check his baggage at the airport?

His trunk wouldn't fit in the overhead compartment!

Where do sheep families go on vacation?

To the BAAAAA-hamas!

Sue: I thought fish didn't go on vacation!

Stu: Why not?!

Sue: They're always in schools! LOL!

Moe: Why do yo-yos go on vacation?

Joe: I give up! Why do yo-yos go on vacation?!

Moe: They need to unwind! :)

Flight attendant: Did you enjoy your flight?

Samantha: Yes, I thought the plane had a good ALT-itude!

Where did the class hamster go on vacation?

HAMSTER-dam!

Teacher: Did you enjoy your trip to the beach?

Student: Yes, the ocean was nice and always WAVED!

Teacher: Did the ocean say anything to you?

Student: Yes, it said, "Long time no SEA!"

Where do superheroes go for summer break?

CAPE Town!

Why did the teacher put her toe in the pool?

She wanted to TEST the water! LOL!

Q: What's black and white and red all over?

A: A zebra that got sunburned on vacation!

Teacher: Did you like going camping?

Student: In was in-TENTS!

Brother: What kind of snack did you get for our flight?

Sister: PLANE chocolate! LOL!

Where does a moose family go for a vacation?

To an a-MOOSE-ment park!

Teacher! Teacher!

Why did the teacher roll his eyes?

His PUPILS were acting up!

Q: Why do teachers always start the day with attendance?

A: They are very ABSENT-minded!

Teacher: When you wrote the alphabet, you skipped one letter.

Student: I can't figure out Y!

Teacher: What's your favorite subject?

Student: Global Studies means the world to me!

What do chickens take in school?

EGGS-aminations!

What did George Washington say after crossing the Delaware?

"Get out of the boat, men!"

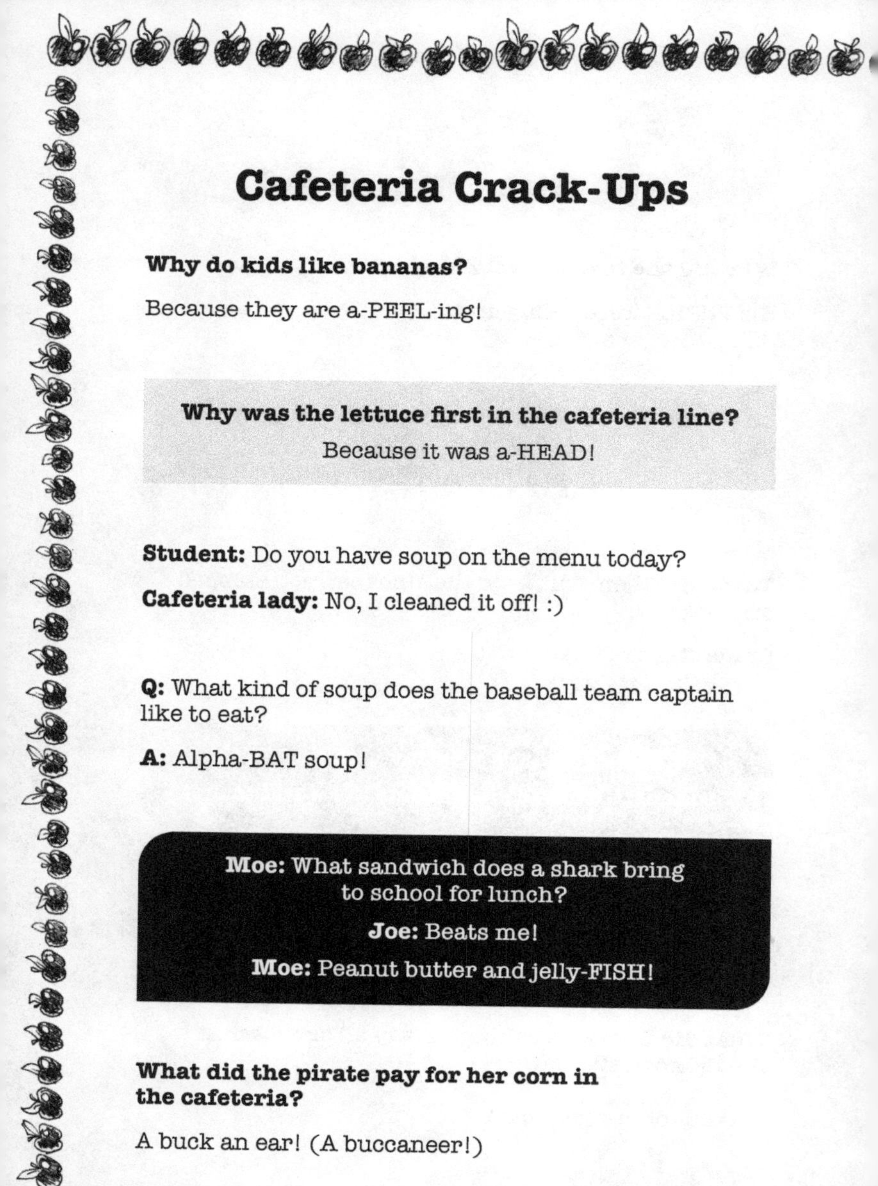

Cafeteria Crack-Ups

Why do kids like bananas?

Because they are a-PEEL-ing!

Why was the lettuce first in the cafeteria line?

Because it was a-HEAD!

Student: Do you have soup on the menu today?

Cafeteria lady: No, I cleaned it off! :)

Q: What kind of soup does the baseball team captain like to eat?

A: Alpha-BAT soup!

Moe: What sandwich does a shark bring to school for lunch?

Joe: Beats me!

Moe: Peanut butter and jelly-FISH!

What did the pirate pay for her corn in the cafeteria?

A buck an ear! (A buccaneer!)

What's the best thing to put in a pie?

Your teeth! LOL!

Teacher: Ethan, your grammar isn't proper.

Ethan: Aw, I ain't gonna be the one to tell 'er!

Sue: What insect gets the best grades in English class?

Lou: It's a mystery to me!

Sue: A spelling bee!

What does the French teacher say when she feeds her dog?

"BONE appetit!"

Music Class Nutty Notes

Moe: Why do hummingbirds hum?

Joe: Search me!

Moe: Because they can't remember the words!

Star students in music class: Amanda Lynn and Claire Annette!

Why did the bee get shooed out of music class?

For STINGING a song!

Ted: Why are pirates good at singing the scales?

Ned: I don't know, why are pirates good at singing the scales?

Ted: Because they hit the high Cs!

Q. Where's the best place to play the piano?

A. In the Baby Grand Canyon!

Q: What kind of music does a burrito love?

A: W-RAP!

Jack: What kind of bird plays the guitar?

Mack: I cannot guess!

Jack: A STR-umming bird! LOL!

Chapter 3

Chuckle with These Books...

Having Fun at the Ocean
by Sandy Shore

Achieve Your Dreams
by Constance Goals

How to Count
by Juan Tutree

Helping the Less Fortunate
by Linda Hand

Learn about Lightbulbs
by Alec Tricity

Dealing with Depression
by Emma Down

Fun with Telescopes
by C. A. Lott

Lunch on the Go
by Sam Widge

The Treasury of Mystery Stories
by Hugh Dunnit

Great Birthday Parties
by Rhoda Ponee

Planning for Your Future
by Iris Formore

When Your Best Friend Moves
by Miles A. Part

Keeping Your Hair Healthy

by Noah Dan Druff

Explore the World of Frogs

by Lilly Pond

Solving Math Problems

by Adam Upp

Never Give Up

by Percy Vear

Dealing with Bug Bites

by Amos Keeto

How to Succeed in Life

by Keith Ontrien

Standing Up to Bullies

by Julie Mealone

How to Enjoy School

by Olive Tulern

Taking Night Classes

by Daisy Sleeps

Gym Class LOLs

Why is Cinderella a crummy basketball player?

She always runs away from balls!

Stan: Emily is the best soccer player and gets good grades, too!

Dan: Yeah, she's always using her HEAD!

Lil: Why do you like playing soccer so much?

Jill: I get a real kick out of it!

Q: Why does a basketball player like donuts?

A: Because she loves to dunk them!

Zoe: Why did the banana sign up for gymnastics?

Zelda: I haven't a clue!

Zoe: She wanted to do BANANA splits! :D

Q: Why are dolphins good at soccer?

A: Because they DIVE a lot!

What's harder to catch the faster you run?

Your BREATH!

Chapter 4

School Sports Sillies

Why is the albatross bad at soccer?

Because he doesn't have two good wings!

Why is the school coach so positive?

He whistles while he works!

Q: What did the outfielder say to the baseball?

A: "I'll catch ya later!" Guffaw!

Moe: Where did you get that cool soccer uniform?

Joe: NEW JERSEY!

Fred: Why is a kangaroo good at basketball?

Ned: Lay it on me!

Fred: They make good JUMP shots! HA! HA!

What move did the pirate make in basketball?

A jump HOOK!

Sue: What runs around the track, but never moves?

Lou: No clue, Sue!

Sue: The FENCE!

Why was the chicken the head cheerleader?

She was good at EGG-ing the team on!

What do you call a biography of a basketball player?

A TALL tale! GO TEAM!

Tim: Why did the baseball player leave the bowling alley?

Jim: He got three strikes and thought he was out!

Why did the basketball player come back early from his family vacation?

He got called for traveling!

Sue: What does the basketball coach like on her sandwich?

Lou: Search me!

Sue: SWISH cheese! LOL!

Q: Why don't butterflies like volleyball?

TA: They are afraid of the NET!

How does the soccer team keep cool?

They stand near the FANS! ;)

Why did the bully quit the soccer team?

He felt bad about kicking the ball around!

How did Cinderella improve her game?

She got a PUMPKIN for a coach!

Wy did the pig get kicked off the basketball team?

He was hogging the ball!

Why did the dog do so well at school?

Because he was the teacher's PET!

Which school subject do runners like most?

Ge-JOG-raphy! LOL!

Share These on the Bus!

What did the student see on the desk in wood shop?

He SAW DUST!

Which is the friendliest school?

HI school!

Where do sharks go for winter break?

FIN-land!

What did the astronaut's mother give her on the way to school?

LAUNCH money!

Fred: Would you like to hear how I learned to tie my shoes in kindergarten?

Ned: I'd rather KNOT!

Which school has the best basketball team?

HEIGHT school!

Which insect gets the best grades in English?

The BOOKWORM!

What does a bull edit?

The school MOOSE-paper! HA! HA! HA!

What did the art teacher say when the students asked her if painting is difficult?

"No, it's EASEL!"

Moe: Why did the chicken cross the playground?

Joe: To get to the other SLIDE!

What do you say to someone who just finished high school?

"Con-GRAD-ulations!"

Which color should a cheerleader's uniform be?

YELL-ow!

Laffy: Which school has the best karate team?

Daffy: HI-YA school!

SUE: Why are you writing with a carrot?

STU: Oh, no! I must have EATEN my PENCIL!

What is the most dangerous thing to order in the school cafeteria?

PIRANHA-INFESTED TOMATO SOUP!

How do you know when an elephant is in your locker?

You can't shut the door!

How does the principal get to school?

On the school BOSS!

Which school band instrument can you use to catch fish?

A clari-NET!

Why did the artist do so well on his test?

He had a STROKE of genius!

Why did the golfer do so well in school?

He was the teacher's PUTT!

What did the straight-A student order in the school cafeteria?

An honor ROLL!

Which kind of sandwiches do temporary teachers eat?

SUBS! :)

What is the school band's favorite month?

MARCH!

Which position would a snowman play on the school baseball team?

FROST base!

What happens when you leave your library books outside overnight?

They become over-DEW! Guffaw!

Teacher: What did Sir Isaac Newton say when he discovered gravity?

Tom: "OUCH!"

Which school has the best football team?

HIKE school!

What is the physical education teacher's name?

Jim Nasium!

How do donkeys get to school every day?

On the MULE bus!

Ticklers!

Why shouldn't you do your homework on an empty stomach?

It's better to use PAPER!

Where does a squirrel write his class assignments?

In a NUT-book!

Tracey: Is it lunchtime?

Teacher: Not for another thirty minutes.

Tracey: Oh, then my stomach must be FAST!

What should you do when your tongue is all red?

Bring it back to the library! LOL!

Which position would a fisherman play on the school baseball team?

CATCHER!

Which position would an elevator play on the school baseball team?

LIFT field! :)

Which position would an orange play on the school baseball team?

RIPE field!

Why did the charge card turn in more homework?

It wanted extra CREDIT!

What is a cow's favorite class?

MOO-sic! LOL!

What does a pig use to take notes?

A PIG pen!

Butter: Did you go someplace for vacation?

Bread: No, I just stayed home and loafed!

Why couldn't the lunch lady find her cooking utensils?

The cat had her TONGS!

What does a dog order in the school cafeteria?

Chicken POODLE soup!

How did the chicken wake up for school?

It used an alarm CLUCK!

Truthful + Monkey = Honest Ape!

What is the school librarian's name?

RITA BOOK! (Read a book!)

Why can't you take an elephant to school?

Because it won't fit in your backpack!

Chapter 5

LOL with Nurse Nancy!

Why did the fish go to the school nurse?

It wasn't feeling WHALE!

Richie: I just sat on a thumbtack!

School nurse: What's the POINT?

Phil: I feel run down!

School nurse: Did you get the license plate number?

Jenny: Why did the apple stay home from school?

Benny: I give up!

Jenny: She was feeling ROTTEN!

School nurse: Where did you get this sting from?

Evan: In third period we had a SPELLING BEE!

Why did the corn go to the school nurse?

It had an EAR-ache!

Student: I swallowed a kazoo in music class!

School nurse: Good thing you weren't playing the TUBA!

Why did the lemon go to the school nurse?

It needed lemon AID!

Why did the sheep go to the school nurse?

She wasn't feeling WOOL!

Why did the small bucket go see the school nurse?

It was looking a little PAIL! LOL!

Chapter 6
RECESS ROAR!

Just for Fun!

Teacher: How do you spell "Washington"?

Lily: The STATE or the PRESIDENT?

What do vultures eat in the afternoon?

An after-school SNAKE!

What is the painting teacher's name?

Art N. Craft!

Why did the piece of corn join the school band?

It had an EAR for music!

Money + Cashew = DOUGH-Nut!

Which sport do yellow jackets play?

Fris-BEE! ROTFL!

Where do cows hang their artwork at school?

On the BULL-etin board!

What sport did the shoe play in school?

SOCK-er!

Why did the music teacher keep her flute in the refrigerator?

She liked COOL music!

What kind of test does a dog take?

A PUP quiz! :D

Spider + Paw = BUG Foot! Ha! Ha!

What is a rattlesnake's favorite school subject?

HISS-tory!

Why did the captain of the track team do so well in English?

He was a SPEED reader!

What do you call the line in the school cafeteria?

The CHEW-CHEW train!

Made You Laff!

What does a skunk order when the cafeteria serves hamburgers?

STENCH fries! LOL!

What does an umbrella order when the cafeteria serves hamburgers?

DRENCH fries!

What does a weightlifter order when the cafeteria serves hamburgers?

BENCH fries! :)

What does a thirsty kid order when the cafeteria serves hamburgers?

QUENCH fries!

School Knock-Knocks

Knock, knock!

Who's there?

Ken!

Ken who?

KEN you drive me to school? I missed the bus!

Knock, knock!

Who's there?

Spell!

Spell who?

W-H-O!

Knock, knock!

Who's there?

Attila!

Attila who?

ATTILA the teacher if you pull my hair again! :D

Knock, knock!

Who's there?

Watson!

Watson who?

WATSON the history test?

Knock, knock!

Who's there?

Alex!

Alex who?

ALEX the teacher if I can get a hall pass!

Knock, knock!

Who's there?

Vera!

Vera who?

VERA rude of you to talk back in class!

Laugh It Up!

What kind of pets do teachers at beauty schools like?

HARES!

Which sport do dogs play in school?

BISCUIT-ball!

Which sport do insects play in school?

BEE-sketball!

Why did the ladder fail his history test?

He got the answers RUNG!

Where does the lunch lady's kitten eat?

In the CAT-eteria!

Tremble + Sharp Stick = SHAKE-SPEAR!

What do you learn from a teacher who teaches health and math classes?

LUNG division!

Phil: What kind of music do geology teachers love?

Bill: I give up, what kind of music do geology teachers love?

Phil: ROCK! HAHAHAHA!

Where does the honor society adviser keep his goldfish?

In a THINK TANK!

Kendall: Why are you going to English class?

Alex: Because the English class won't come to me! :)

What do you say when the lunch lady gives you a hot dog?

"FRANKS a lot!" LOL!

Where can you find a cow's class picture?

In a STEER-book!

Where can you find a fawn's class picture?

In a DEER-book!

Did You Hear This One?

What do turtles give in pop quizzes?

SNAPPY answers!

Fowl + Dog + Broth = Chicken POODLE Soup!

Why did the members of the tennis team get jobs in the cafeteria?

They were good at SERVING!

What is a dog's favorite school subject?

ARF class!

What has two hundred feet and sings?

The school CHOIR! ROTFL!

What did the mollusk bring to its teacher?

A CRAB apple!

Who is an English teacher's favorite relative?

His GRAMMAR!

Bill: How did the class rabbit get to the seashore?

Lill: He HOPPED on a plane!

Bill: What kind of plane?

Lill: A HARE-plane!

Teacher: If you multiplied 4,876 by 6,345 what would you get?

Student: The WRONG answer!

What's louder than a cheerleader?

TWO cheerleaders!

What does a pig do after school?

HAM work!

Yellow Veggie + Police Officer =

Corn on the COP!

Gary: What color should I paint the cat's picture?

Art teacher: PURR-ple!

Where do cows go on class trips?

To the MOO-seum!

Funny You Should Ask!

What tool is good at math?

Multi-PLIERS!

How do you get into the music appreciation class?

Through the BACH door!

Knock, knock!

Who's there?

Tennesse!

Tennesse who?

TENNESSE sum of five plus five!

Why couldn't the piano teacher open the door to his classroom?

Because all the KEYS were inside!

Why did the pair of scissors become a cool bus driver?

It knew a lot of short-CUTS!

What is a school librarian's favorite food?

Ma-SHHH-ed potatoes! ROTFL!

What does a deer use to carry her books?

A BUCK-pack!

Why is a book like a watermelon?

Because on the inside it's RED!

Peg: Did you hear that the teacher's cat is crabby?

Meg: Yeah, it's a SOUR-puss!

What game do kangaroos love to play at recess?

HOP-scotch!

Foot + Thirteen-Wheeler = TOE Truck!

On what day do they serve fish in the cafeteria?

FRY-day!

Which animal is found in the alphabet?

EWE!

Which two animals are found in the alphabet?

Double EWE! ;)

What did the sore back get on its report card?

Straight ACHES! ROTFL!

Gary: Did you hear the letter A has perfect attendance?

Larry: Why no, Gary, I didn't!

Gary: Yeah, it's always in CL-A-SS! Get it?!?!

Larry: Why yes, Gary, but it was so funny I forgot to laugh!

What should you do when the cafeteria serves blueberries?

Try to CHEER them UP!

Body of Water + Cutting Tool = SEA SAW! Guffaw!

Why did the cat join the school band?

Because it loves MEOW-sic!

What kind of boats do college students sail on?

Scholar-SHIPS!

English teacher: A, B, C, D, E, F, G, H, I, J... What comes after J?

Rachael: WALKING! LOL!

Chapter 7

Riddle Me This!

What does the school coach use to clean his clothes?

The school BLEACH-ers!

Where did the queen bee go to school?

BUZZ-ness school!

What did the school janitor order at the hotel?

BROOM service!

What do dogs wear when they play football in gym class?

Hel-MUTTS! ROTFL!

Which letter is always asking questions?

Y! Guffaw!

What is a waiter's favorite part of a school basketball game?

The TIP-off! :)

What sport does the geometry teacher like?

FIGURE skating!

Teacher: You really need to learn decimals!

Tom: What's the POINT?

What does a baseball coach keep on his doorstep?

A MITT!

Larry: Teacher, I don't have my homework because a ten-foot tall lion ate it!

Teacher: That's some LYIN'!

Butterfly + Arithmetic = MOTH-ematics!

What does a snowman eat when the cafeteria serves Mexican food?

BRR-itos!

What do you need to take to get into dental school?

An ORAL exam! HA HA HA!

Money + Scram = Cash-SHOO!

Geography teacher: Which state is the most curious?

Luke: Ha-WHY-ii!

Willy: I keep thinking we have a test today!

Lilly: We DO have a test today!

Willy: I know. That's why I keep THINKING it!

What kind of ice cream did the snake order in the school cafeteria?

ASP-berry!

Geography teacher: Which city is really odd?

Bob: Albu-QUIRKY!

Try Not to Laugh!

Biology teacher: What do snakes have that no other reptiles have?

Sally: BABY snakes!

How does a swimmer get to school?

In a car-POOL!

Knock, knock!

Who's there?

Justin!

Justin who?

JUSTIN TIME for art class!

What does a music teacher play on an electric guitar?

Electric CORDS!

Why did the tongue stay up late?

Because it was cramming for its TASTE test!

Why did the shoelace get sent to the principal's office?

It was acting KNOTTY!

What kind of test does a cheerleader take?

A PEP quiz!

What kind of vehicle does a math teacher drive?

A 4 x 4! ROTFL!

Bruno: I want to be a farmer when I grow up!

School counselor: That's a GROWING FIELD!

What was the elevator's school year like?

It had a lot of UPs and DOWNs!

Which state did the geography teacher say is the tiniest?

MINI-sota!

What do penguins order in the cafeteria?

Iceberg-ERS!

Mary: I heard you have to go to court!

Gary: Yeah, I'm taking a TENNIS CLASS! LOL!

Geography teacher: Which state has the biggest phone bill?

Abner: CALL-ifornia! HA HA HA!

If I Make the Team...

Stella: If I make the tumbling team, I'm gonna FLIP!

Sara: If I make the basketball team, I'm gonna have a BALL!

Tom: If I make the baseball team, I'm gonna go BATTY!

Ethan: If I make the debate team, I'll be SPEECHLESS!

Michael: If I make the track team, I'll have overcome a BIG HURDLE!

Kathy: If I make the soccer team, I'll have achieved my GOALS!

Eric: If I make the hockey team, I'll STICK to it!

Donna: If I make the skating team, that would be ICE! :D

Bill: If I make the golf team, that would be a HOLE lot of fun!

Danielle: If I make the tennis team, I'll raise a RACKET!

Andrew: If I make the bowling team, I'll have no time to SPARE!

Jennifer: If I make the swim team, I'll make a BIG SPLASH!

Jason: If I make the football team, I'll have to PASS!

Lynn: If I make the volleyball team, I'll JUMP for joy!

Taking Attendance

Teacher: John Barber!

John Barber: HAIR!

Teacher: Billy Rabbit!

Billy Rabbit: HARE!

Teacher: Larry Laugh!

Larry Laugh: HAR!

Teacher: E.R. Lobe!

E.R. Lobe: HEAR!

Teacher: Em Ployer!

Em Ployer: HIRE! :D

I Made a Funny

What do you call someone who's good at geometry and sports?

A MATH-lete!

Fourteen Karats + Flounder = Gold-FISH!

What did the ice cream cone get at graduation?

A DIP-loma!

Why did the chauffeur do so well in school?

He had a lot of DRIVE! ROTFL!

Science teacher: What do you call the hair on a giraffe's tail?

Kathy: Giraffe HAIR!

Why did the boy ride his bike to school?

Because it was too heavy to carry!

Science teacher: What kind of ant is gray?

Luke: An ELEPH-ant!

What happened when the math teacher tripped and fell?

He FRACTIONED his ARM!

Why did the principal cross the road?

Because it was the CHICKEN'S DAY OFF! ROTFL!

More Geography Guffaws

Geography teacher: What is a lion's favorite state?

Giuliano: MAINE!

Geography teacher: Which state is the loudest?

Grace: Illi-NOISE! ;)

Geography teacher: Which is a train's favorite state?

Theresa: Massa-CHOO-CHOO-setts!

Geography teacher: Which state makes the most sandwiches?

Griffin: DELI-ware!

Geography teacher: Which state uses the most straws?

Robin: Minne-SODA!

Geography teacher: Which city wanders around aimlessly?

Brenda: ROME!

Laughing Out Loud!

What does a radiator eat when the school cafeteria serves Mexican food?

Fa-HEAT-as!

Which state did the geography teacher say has the most bills?

I-OWE-a!

Beth: When do I have to turn in my report on condensation?

Science teacher: In DEW time!

Which type of snake is on the front of a school bus?

A windshield VIPER!

Which kind of books do racecar drivers read in school?

AUTO-biographies! ROTFL!

What is a history teacher's favorite fruit?

DATES! :)

Which state sells the most school supplies?

PENCIL-vania!

Mack: What's a lion's favorite thing to do at recess?

Jack: If I only knew!

Mack: Climb the JUNGLE gym!

What did the baby birds do before the school football game?

They had a PEEP rally!

More School Knock Knocks

Knock, knock!

Who's there?

Fred!

Fred who?

FRED I failed my test!

Knock, knock!

Who's there?

Harry!

Harry who?

HARRY UP! The school bus is coming!

Knock, knock!

Who's there?

Scott!

Scott who?

SCOTT an A on my science project!

Knock, knock!

Who's there?

Orange juice!

Orange juice who?

ORANGE JUICE glad I'm home from school?

Knock, knock!

Who's there?

Wanda!

Wanda who?

WANDA go to the prom with me? :D

Knock, knock!

Who's there?

Bern!

Bern who?

BERN lunch? The cafeteria smells!

Knock, knock!

Who's there?

Ivan!

Ivan who?

IVAN history test third period!

Chapter 8

Class Clownies

Which state did the geography teacher say you can walk on?

FLOOR-ida!

What day did the automobile fender visit school?

CAR REAR day! :)

Mon: How do you like your astronomy class?

Tom: It's looking up!

Which state did the geography teacher say takes the most showers?

WASH-ington!

Which state did the geography teacher say is a pig's favorite?

New PORK!

Knock, knock!

Who's there?

Olive!

Olive who?

OLIVE next door, wanna walk to school together? LOL!

Which state is an art teacher's favorite?

COLOR-ado!

Tim: How do you spell "ISSISSIPPI"?

Teacher: Do you mean "Mississippi"?

Tim: No, I already wrote the letter "M"!

Which state did the geography teacher say has the most dirty laundry?

New HAMPER-shire!

What kind of shoes does the English teacher's pet wear?

Open TOAD!

Jack: And who is a chicken's favorite composer?

Mack: Tell me, please!

Jack: BACH! BACH! BACH!

Teddy: We learned how to write in school today!

Mom: Really? What did you write?

Teddy: I don't know, we haven't learned to READ yet!

How long do you have arithmetic class?

A SUM-mester! Guffaw!

What's weirder than a talking dog?

A SPELLING BEE!

Teacher: Give me an example of an interrogative sentence.

Elina: Me?

Teacher: Good!

Fred: I'm going to join the chess club. It meets at KNIGHT!

Which state did the geography teacher say has the most acorns?

OAK-lahoma!

Chapter 9

Even More School Knock-Knocks

Knock, knock!

Who's there?

Rhea!

Rhea who?

RHEA chapters one through nine for homework tonight!

Knock, knock!

Who's there?

Dewey!

Dewey who?

DEWEY have any homework tonight? ;D

Knock, knock!

Who's there?

Drew!

Drew who?

DREW a picture in art class today. Wanna see it?

Knock, knock!

Who's there?

Tamara!

Tamara who?

TAMARA we'll be having a test!

Knock, knock!

Who's there?

Ester!

Ester who?

ESTER a way I can get extra credit?

Knock, knock!

Who's there?

Abbey!

Abbey who?

ABBEY, C, D, E, F, G!

Knock, knock!

Who's there?

Martian!

Martian who?

MARTIAN band!

Knock, knock!

Who's there?

Rita!

Rita who?

RITA good book lately?

Knock, knock!

Who's there?

Pat!

Pat who?

PAT me on the back! Just got an A on my test!

LOL!

What did the bee do during study hall?

BUZZY work! LOL!

What kind of cookie did the lunch lady bake for her pet bird?

Chocolate CHIRP! :D

Why do lamps do so well in school?

Because they're so BRIGHT! :D

What does it say on the principal's office door?

Princi-PULL!

What does a librarian wear on her feet?

...SHHH-oes!

Which pet plays in the marching band?

A trum-PET!

Teacher: Spell "MOUSETRAP."

Rob: C-A-T!

Booker: Do you have any cookbooks?

School librarian: You're looking for stirring stories?

Chapter 10
Puns from the Principal

Funny Bones!

Mom: Why couldn't the pancake go to school?

Dad: She had a WAFFLE cold! :)

Why were the glue and the scotch tape best friends?

They always STUCK together!

What does a foot eat when the cafeteria serves Mexican food?

Burri-TOES!

What does a dog play in the school band?

The trom-BONE!

English teacher: I cannot give you an A on your essay on marathon running.

Student: Why not?

English teacher: There were too many RUN-ON SENTENCES!

Grace: What's a pirate's fave subject?

Griffin: ARRRRRT!

Principal: Why did you quit teaching your history class?

Teacher: I didn't see any future in it!

Art student: I can't find the glue!

Art teacher: STICK to it!

Why did the kid bring a jump rope to school?

The teacher said she was doing well and could SKIP the math test!

Mom: Why did the girl take a ladder to school?

Dad: She was going to HIGH school!

Hip: How was your math test?

Hop: The questions were easy!

Hip: Yay!

Hop: Yeah, but the answers were HARD!

Kid: I'm glad you named me Grace!

Parent: Why?

Kid: Because that's what the teacher calls me!

First pig: Oink!

Second pig: Moo-oo!

First pig: What do you mean "Moo-oo!"?

Second pig: To graduate I have to learn a FOREIGN LANGUAGE!

Mom: Do you like your new math teacher?

Griffin: Yes, but she has a lot of PROBLEMS!

Dad: Grace, do you like your new geology teacher?

Grace: Yes, but he has ROCKS in his head!

Why do teachers wear sunglasses?

Because their students are so BRIGHT!

Q: Where do you go to open doors?

A: The Florida KEYS!

About the Author

Vice magazine has called Yoe the "Indiana Jones of comics historians." *Publisher Weekly* says he's the "archivist of the ridiculous and the sublime" and calls his work "brilliant." *The Onion* calls him a "celebrated designer," *The Library Journal* says, "a comics guru." BoingBoing hails him "a fine cartoonist and a comic book historian of the first water." Yoe was creative director/vice president/general manager of Jim Henson's Muppets, and a creative director at Nickelodeon and Disney. Craig has won multiple Eisner Awards and the Gold Medal from the Society of Illustrators.

Mango Publishing, established in 2014, publishes an eclectic list of books by diverse authors—both new and established voices—on topics ranging from business, personal growth, women's empowerment, LGBTQ studies, health, and spirituality to history, popular culture, time management, decluttering, lifestyle, mental wellness, aging, and sustainable living. We were recently named 2019's #1 fastest growing independent publisher by Publishers Weekly. Our success is driven by our main goal, which is to publish high quality books that will entertain readers as well as make a positive difference in their lives.

Our readers are our most important resource; we value your input, suggestions, and ideas. We'd love to hear from you—after all, we are publishing books for you!

Please stay in touch with us and follow us at:

Facebook: Mango Publishing

Twitter: @MangoPublishing

Instagram: @MangoPublishing

LinkedIn: Mango Publishing

Pinterest: Mango Publishing

Sign up for our newsletter at www.mangopublishinggroup.com and receive a free book!

Join us on Mango's journey to reinvent publishing, one book at a time.

HA!
HA!
HA!
HA!
HA! HA!
HA!
HEE!
HA!
HO!
HA!
ROTFL!
HA!
LOL!
SCHOOL BUS
LOL!
LAUGH!
OUT!
LOUD!
HA!
HA!
HA!
HA!
HA!
HA! HA!
HA!
HEE!
HA!
HO!
HA!
ROTFL!
HA!
LOL!
SCHOOL BUS
LOL!
LAUGH!
OUT!
LOUD!
HA!